TRENDS IN SOUTHEAST ASIA

NAQUIB AL-ATTAS' ISLAMIZATION OF KNOWLEDGE

Its Impact on Malay Religious Life, Literature, Language and Culture

Mohd Faizal Musa

ISSUE

16

2021

 YUSOF ISHAK INSTITUTE

Published by: ISEAS Publishing
                30 Heng Mui Keng Terrace
                Singapore 119614
                publish@iseas.edu.sg
                http://bookshop.iseas.edu.sg

ISEAS Library Cataloguing-in-Publication Data

Name(s): Mohd Faizal Musa, author.
Title: Naquib Al-Attas' Islamization of knowledge : its impact on Malay religious life, literature, language and culture / by Mohd Faizal Musa.
Description: Singapore : ISEAS–Yusof Ishak Institute, July 2021. | Series: Trends in Southeast Asia, ISSN 0219-3213 ; TRS16/21 | Includes bibliographical references.
Identifiers: ISBN 9789815011081 (soft cover) | ISBN 9789815011098 (pdf)
Subjects: LCSH: Knowledge, Theory of (Islam). | Malays (Asian people)—Religious life—Malaysia. | Religion and culture—Malaysia. | Religion and state—Malaysia.
Classification: LCC DS501 I59T no. 16(2021)

Typeset by Superskill Graphics Pte Ltd
Printed in Singapore by Mainland Press Pte Ltd

FOREWORD

The economic, political, strategic and cultural dynamism in Southeast Asia has gained added relevance in recent years with the spectacular rise of giant economies in East and South Asia. This has drawn greater attention to the region and to the enhanced role it now plays in international relations and global economics.

The sustained effort made by Southeast Asian nations since 1967 towards a peaceful and gradual integration of their economies has had indubitable success, and perhaps as a consequence of this, most of these countries are undergoing deep political and social changes domestically and are constructing innovative solutions to meet new international challenges. Big Power tensions continue to be played out in the neighbourhood despite the tradition of neutrality exercised by the Association of Southeast Asian Nations (ASEAN).

The **Trends in Southeast Asia** series acts as a platform for serious analyses by selected authors who are experts in their fields. It is aimed at encouraging policymakers and scholars to contemplate the diversity and dynamism of this exciting region.

THE EDITORS

Series Chairman:
   Choi Shing Kwok

Series Editor:
   Ooi Kee Beng

Editorial Committee:
   Daljit Singh
   Francis E. Hutchinson
   Norshahril Saat

Naquib Al-Attas' Islamization of Knowledge: Its Impact on Malay Religious Life, Literature, Language and Culture

By Mohd Faizal Musa

EXECUTIVE SUMMARY

- The concept of the Islamization of knowledge was introduced by Syed Muhammad Naquib Al-Attas in the late 1970s. It aimed to detach knowledge from Western culture and civilization in order to replace it with Islamic concepts, frameworks and values.
- The Islamization of knowledge was to occur in the fields of education and culture, manifesting in changes to the syllabus in institutions of higher learning and niche areas of interest in selected research institutes. In the field of culture, however, it resulted in an unintended consequence of Malay literature being heavily characterized by Islamic elements.
- Over the years, proponents of the Islamization of knowledge in Malaysia have moved beyond the fields of education and culture. They have entered the mainstream and become part of the state machinery, thus possibly impacting national policies.
- The concept has also evolved and arguably led to the strengthening of Islamic conservatism among Malaysian intellectual and cultural elites.
- More specifically, its exclusivist thinking does not augur well for intra- and intercommunal relations in the country.

Naquib Al-Attas' Islamization of Knowledge: Its Impact on Malay Religious Life, Literature, Language and Culture

By Mohd Faizal Musa[1]

INTRODUCTION

Syed Muhammad Naquib Al-Attas (born 1931) is a Malaysian thinker who is world-renowned in the academic world and in the field of arts and culture. He received his higher education at the Royal Military Academy in Sandhurst, and later at McGill University in Montreal as well as the School of Oriental and African Studies (SOAS) in London. His early writings mainly revolved around Sufism, and his most monumental work is *The Mysticism of Hamzah Fansuri* (1970). His other influential works include *The Origin of the Malay Sha'ir* (1968), *The Correct Date of the Terengganu Inscription* (1972), and *Prolegomena to the Metaphysics of Islam: An Exposition of the Fundamental Elements of the Worldview of Islam* (1995). He is also known for his eye for design and his skill in calligraphy, having founded and designed the building of the International Institute of Islamic Thought and Civilization (ISTAC) in Kuala Lumpur, which was officially opened in 1991.

It is common knowledge that the institute receives large funding from the Malaysian government and enjoys political support from the former president of the Malaysian Islamic Youth Movement (ABIM), and former deputy prime minister, Anwar Ibrahim. As Chandra Muzaffar (1987, p. 54) noted, "the person who had the greatest influence upon

---

[1] Mohd Faizal Musa is Visiting Fellow at the ISEAS – Yusof Ishak Institute, Singapore and Research Fellow at the Institute of the Malay World and Civilization, National University of Malaysia (UKM).

Anwar Ibrahim in his ABIM years was Syed Naquib Al-Attas, then Professor of Malay Literature at Universiti Kebangsaan Malaysia (UKM)." This was further highlighted by Mona Abaza (1999, p. 189) in her article "Intellectuals, Power and Islam in Malaysia: S.N. Al-Attas or the Beacon on the Crest of a Hill", where she referred to Al-Attas as Anwar's "intellectual mentor". According to Komaruddin Sassi (2020, pp. 53–54) who wrote his doctoral thesis on Al-Attas, it was Anwar who appointed him as the first occupant of the Abu Hamid Al-Ghazali Chair of Islamic Thought at ISTAC.

Beyond Anwar, Al-Attas had a wide impact on student movements and education in Malaysia in the 1970s, especially within the context of Islamic revivalism at the time. As Abaza put it, "his impact on the student movement of the seventies is substantial in reviving Islamic culture and rationalizing Sufism. If the early Al-Attas interpreted Hamzah Fansuri as a reformer and a rebellious Sufi thinker, ISTAC incorporated traits of 'refeudalization' and the institutionalization of an Islam of power" (Abaza 1999, p. 216).

It can be argued that since its establishment, ISTAC has created a group of followers of Al-Attas who can be described as elitist. In a book on the development of Parti Islam Se-Malaysia (PAS), Farish A. Noor (2004, p. 546) stated that "Syed Naquib Al-Attas' dominant stature and intellectual acumen were precisely the factors that made ISTAC an impenetrable and inaccessible institution", and that the books that he published and ideas that the staff of the institute were interested in were "well beyond the reach of the ordinary masses". Some of the ideas they were interested in included philosophical Sufism and historical dating methods as opposed to concrete issues such as corruption and feudalism which affected Malaysian Muslims at various levels. Furthermore, Komaruddin Sassi (2020, p. 259) criticized Al-Attas for neglecting novel ideas and wisdom from contemporary Muslim intellectuals and found him unappreciative of others even though Islam promotes the maxim of keeping the best from the past and taking what is good of the new.[2]

---

[2] In Arabic, "*al-muhafazah 'ala al-qadim al-salih wa al-akhadh bi al-jadid al-aslah*". Komaruddin Sassi went as far as saying that Al-Attas is too self-evident, self-sufficient, and tends to flatter himself (2020, pp. 280–81).

Yet, despite his detachment from the masses, Al-Attas' contributions led him to be regarded by his students, followers and fans as someone unparalleled in authority. In an inaugural lecture upon his appointment as professor at Universiti Malaya (UM), Hashim Haji Musa (2006, p. 79), a renowned sociolinguist and specialist in Malay studies, referred to Al-Attas as a "contemporary reformist" who "holds strongly to the pure values of Islam" and whose enforcement and mobilization of the religion was highly recognized. He said that Al-Attas was responsible for "positioning Islam as the main foundation in Malay studies, and subsequently spearheaded the movement of Islamizing science and education" with the establishment of ISTAC. Furthermore, he highlighted that because Al-Attas "disputed and dismissed Abdullah Munshi's reputation as the pioneer or father of modern Malay literature", the impact of this opinion gave Islam an overly special position in Malay literature, to the extent that it changed the entire cultural landscape and led to the rejection of literature that was considered un-Islamic.

Al-Attas' Islamization of knowledge amounted to the de-Westernizing of knowledge, or the detaching of knowledge from Western culture and civilization, in favour of Islamic concepts, values and worldview (Al-Attas 1978, pp. 131–32). This was to be done through education and the field of culture. This paper discusses the impact of Al-Attas' Islamization of knowledge since its introduction in the 1970s and shows how it has affected the discourse surrounding Islam's role in Malaysian history and society. With full government support, Al-Attas was "committed to providing an Islamic response to the intellectual and cultural challenges of the modern world" (Milner 2011, pp. 218–19).

I will examine the origins of this idea and how it has manifested itself in the fields of education and culture in Malaysia. I argue that Al-Attas' ideas on the Islamization of knowledge could be one of the reasons for the turn towards Islamic conservatism among Malaysian intellectual and cultural elites, and that it has been used to justify certain forms of discrimination against non-Malays and non-Muslims. Some of his ideas were applied even in ways that diverged from their original intent. I will also examine his position on secularism, modern human rights and the role of Islam, and how these impact Malaysian society.

ISLAMIZATION AS RESPONSE TO THE CONTESTED INFLUENCE OF HINDU-BUDDHIST CULTURE

Al-Attas is well known for his negative views on the role of Hindu-Buddhist culture in pre-Islamic Malay society. According to Komaruddin Sassi (2020, pp. 74–76), Al-Attas rejects autochthony in that he denies the influence of Hindu-Buddhist culture in pre-Islamic Malay life and society, and he claims its influence to have been only restricted to the aesthetic realm. In the context of Malay society, autochthony would refer to the argument of Western orientalists or historians that the acceptance of Islam among Malays was facilitated by specific doctrines in Hinduism and Buddhism which had similarities to variants of Islamic mysticism. While Al-Attas' intention in rejecting autochthony was to uphold Islam and Malay culture,[3] his followers—not necessarily his direct students—play down Malay civilization's pre-Islamic past, and neglect the contribution of Hinduism and Buddhism to Malay intellectual life. This has elicited criticisms from scholars, especially those from the hard sciences, of serious oversimplifications of the pre-Islamic past of the Malays.[4]

---

[3] On 18 August 1971, Syed Muhammad Naquib Al-Attas was appointed as Professor at UKM. He presented a main paper at the National Culture Congress that year, titled "Nilai-Nilai Kebudayaan Dalam Bahasa dan Kesusasteraan Melayu: Rumusan Usul-Usul Ilmiah" ("Cultural Values in Malay Language and Literature: Summary of Scientific Suggestions") at UM. His views did not sit well with Malaysian Chinese and Indians. See Mohamed Mustafa Ishak (1999), pp. 139–49. Mohamed also added that many scholars and cultural activists were not invited to the congress, and this was especially the case with Malaysian leftists. For instance, Abdul Samad Ismail, a veteran journalist known for his leftist ideas, contested that the congress was dominated by right-wing Malay nationalists (ibid, p. 139).

[4] Al-Attas' views on pre-Islamic Malay culture goes beyond simply making the case for the significant historical impact and contributions of Islamization on Malay culture and language. In criticizing Orientalists for their attention to Hindu-Buddhist culture, Al-Attas had argued against an autochthonous viewpoint and in the process put pre-Islamic culture and beliefs in a negative light. This argument drew responses from many scholars. For example, a well-known Malaysian

Thus, in order to counteract those who highlight the significance of Hindu-Buddhist culture in pre-Islamic Malay civilization, Al-Attas proposed Islamization. As laid out in his book *Islam and Secularism*, Al-Attas defined Islamization as "the liberation of man first from magical, mythological, animistic, national-cultural tradition opposed to Islam, and then from secular control over his reason and his language" (1978, p. 41). In proposing Islamization, he was weaving Islam and Malay identity into one. As Mona Abaza (1999, p. 209) put it, Al-Attas' act of focusing on Islam at the expense of Hindu-Buddhist elements was an "ideological reconstruction that is co-opted within the official ideology of 'Malayness,' closely interwoven with a new rising Islamic consciousness." Thus, while Islam has often been associated with the Malay identity and while the very definition of "Malay" in the Constitution is connected to Islam, Al-Attas' efforts went beyond highlighting this lived reality.[5] This was symbolized in the functioning of ISTAC, an institution "run in an

---

mathematician, Shaharir Mohamad Zin, along with his students, responded to Al-Attas with a plethora of research on scientific achievements made by Malays before the arrival of Islam, thus debunking Al-Attas' argument that only Islam brought civilization to the Malay world. See, for example, Shaharir Mohamad Zain (2000, 2003); Shaharir Mohamad Zain and Zahrin Affandi Mohd Zahrin, (2019). Many of Shaharir's works aim to correct the misperception that Malays lacked scientific knowledge and logic before the coming of Islam. Shaharir and his followers however are not hostile towards Al-Attas and his students and followers. This could be due to the fact that Shaharir and his students were from the social sciences while Al-Attas was in the humanities. For more on the views of Shaharir and his students, see their collection of essays in Mohd Hazim Shah Abdul Murad (2009). It is also worth mentioning that renowned Malaysian sociologist Abdul Rahman Embong (2002) argued that Al-Attas' view on the superficiality of the Indianization of Malay culture is still inconclusive: "Whether the Indianization thesis has been unduly favoured is still inconclusive and it is up to the historians to verify. Be that as it may, it is a historical fact that Indian influence lasted for many centuries in the Malay world, with Hindu-Buddhist artifacts still to be found today and with many Sanskrit words enriching the Malay vocabulary and lexicography." See Abdul Rahman Embong (2002), p. 42.

[5] In a reader's letter to *Malaysiakini*, Aqil Fithri stated that the issue of Malay supremacy is not something that is generally known: "In its modern history, Malaysia supposedly originated from the idea of *Melayu-Islam*. In fact, this is

authoritarian manner" and that utilized the "manipulation of religious symbols" to achieve "bureaucratization and the reconstruction of the political culture of the Nation-State" (Abaza 1999, p. 216).

Al-Attas' definition of Islamization as provided above has become a reference for many and he is highly regarded for his efforts on that front. For example, Najibah Abdul Mutalib (2000, p. 71) stated that Al-Attas "was one of the many Muslim intellectuals who criticized modern Western science or knowledge. From this criticism was born what has been termed the Islamization of knowledge or the de-Westernization of knowledge. He was one of the first Muslim figures who attempted to give a clear definition of the concept of the process of Islamization." Similarly, Farish Noor (2004, p. 488) has referred to *Islam and Secularism* as Al-Attas' "most influential book ... and it became the standard reference for an entire generation of middle-class professionals, politicians, students and teachers in the country."

AL-ATTAS' ATTITUDE TOWARDS SECULARISM AND MODERN HUMAN RIGHTS

I argue that while Al-Attas proposed Islamization as an antidote to autochthony, he also envisioned it as a rejection of secularism.[6] Al-

---

an intellectual idea which was conceived by Syed Muhammad Naquib Al-Attas before it was elevated by UMNO as a national political idea. Then, the soul of Malaysia that formed was often reliant upon *Melayu-Islam*, while coated with the saying 'also appreciates other races'." See Aqil Fithri (2010). I agree with his view. Although Al-Attas did not use the term "*Ketuanan Melayu*" or Malay supremacy in his 1971 presentation, the spirit of this idea was laid in his paper, hinting at a racial and cultural hierarchy. For instance, according to Al-Attas (1971, p. 8), there should be three defining characteristics for Malaysian society. These were religion, language, and history, or what he called political fate. These three characteristics would form the basis for Islamization (Al-Attas 1971, p. 8).

[6] Al-Attas stated that "the term secularism is meant to denote not merely secular ideologies such as, for example, Communism or Socialism in its various forms, but encompasses also all expressions of the secular worldview including that projected by secularization, which is none other than a secular historical relativism which I have called secularizationism." See Al-Attas (1978), p. 45.

Attas had first denounced secularism in *Risalah untuk Kaum Muslimin* (*Pamphlet for Muslims*) which was first published in 1973, after which he further developed his ideas on the matter, which culminated in the publication of *Islam and Secularism*.[7] However, his definition of Islamization as provided above did not take into account the socio-political factors which characterized post-independence Malaysia, and instead appeared to ignore the complex diversity and plurality of Malaysian society. In the final pages of his book, Al-Attas further stated:

> The man of Islam is he whose reason and language are no longer controlled by magic, myth, superstition, animism, his own cultural and national traditions opposed to Islam and secularism. What I meant when I referred to Westernization seen solely from the perspective of a cultural phenomenon as being a continuation of the Islamization process referred in fact to the general effect Westernization had in the disintegration of the magical world view of the Malay-Indonesian. Islam had already initiated the process of that disintegration, and Westernization continued that process, which is not completely accomplished yet (1978, p. 174).[8]

---

[7] If one were to read this book alongside *Islam and Secularism*, it can be observed that his criticism and perhaps even condemnation of secularism and human rights appears to be more direct in the former, which was written in Malay, as opposed to the latter, which was written in English.

[8] Al-Attas also talked about how "deislamization" had affected the Malay world: "the best specimen of this breed among the tribes that possess no *adab* is to be found in abundance in Malaysia and Indonesia where systematic deislamization has been implemented since colonial days, and where the momentum of secularization is more pronounced than in other parts of the Muslim world. Here perhaps, in the predominantly Islamic region of Southeast Asia, the loss of *adab* due to ignorance of Islam and its world view, as a religion and a civilization, is at a more advanced stage than elsewhere in the Muslim world particularly among the secular Muslim scholars and intellectuals. This state of affairs is due partly to the fact that the process of Islamization began to take effect at a relatively later date than in other Muslim regions, and that Islamization has been interrupted by the arrival of Western colonialism and cultural imperialism. Moreover, the bulk of the *'ulama* are equally immersed in loss of *adab*, seeing that they are the blind followers of the modernists as well as the traditionalists" (1978, pp. 119–20).

Wan Mohd Nor Wan Daud, a former student of Al-Attas who is now regarded as an expert on the latter's ideas, had also stated that Al-Attas rejected the teachings of humanism in referring to them as "the embodiment of the ideology of secularism which diverts the evaluation of everything to the human mind". Al-Attas viewed modern human rights, the rational mind, and the freedom of thought—all of which were related to equality—as "foreign thinking". Additionally, socialism and democracy were also looked upon as sources of confusion for Muslims, as they may think that such notions were parallel with certain dimensions of Islam. The long excerpt below, taken from his discussion on the influence of Western civilization on Muslim minds, is important proof of this line of thought (Al-Attas 2001; pp. 158–59):

> Foreign modes of thinking which have been nurtured in his mind then become increasingly ingrained in the minds of followers and among others and most importantly include:
>
> (1) the understanding of the primacy and superiority of the animal mind, i.e. reason which stems from ratio, in exploring truth and reality, and the primacy of the animal self. This then leads to the understanding of:
> (2) human freedom i.e. the individual self, which also tends to attribute itself to animals, i.e. freedom and liberty, to decide its own fate; to present their own opinions and views. This is closely related to the understanding that:
> (3) human rights strengthens (1) and (2) above. This then leads to the understanding of:
> (4) the equality of human beings, i.e. equality and egalitarianism in the framework of society and the state in terms of man-made laws. Understandings such as these all certainly imply the acceptance of the understanding of:
> (5) human evolution and the history of the world, i.e. evolution—the natural forces which drive towards change for the better, towards purity and also constantly changing so as to continuously embody other forms of perfection. Then with the influence of victory and achievement comes

the understanding of socialism in Western countries, coupled with:

(6) Western socialism as well as its democracy as understood and confused with Islamic understandings of society and politics by some intellectuals of the modernist stream and also others.

Over the years, Al-Attas and his followers consistently promoted his idea of Islamization, while alienating secularism and human rights. However, it must be stated that Al-Attas was against a specific civilizational understanding of human rights based on Western values of secularism and individualism, and not human rights and equality per se. Despite this, he did not present his own conceptualization of human rights, in Islamized form or not. Furthermore, what he presented was what is perceived as cultural relativism in the discourse on human rights.[9]

This approach towards Islamization and the rejection of secularism was also adopted by political parties in the race to out-Islamize one another. For example, Abdul Razak Ayub (1985, pp. 30–37), a well-known journalist in the 1980s whose writings were influential among members of ABIM and PAS, cited Al-Attas' ideas to prove that PAS was the better party. He argued that before the arrival of Islam, Malays were "idol worshippers" and only became rational upon their exposure to Islam. He said that Islam had made Malays superior, but that the colonizers introduced the process of secularization which therefore affected Islamization. In a book titled *Perpecahan Bangsa Melayu* (*The Split of the Malay Race*), Abdul Razak affixed Islam to PAS while the United Malays National Organization (UMNO) was portrayed as a beneficiary of the secularism which the British brought. Unsurprisingly, he did not mention that Al-Attas had spent his younger days living with his uncle, Onn Bin Jaafar, who was one of the founders of UMNO (Komaruddin Sassi 2020, pp. 44–45), and that Al-Attas also had a close

---

[9] I have refuted the claim that Islam rejects modern human rights. See Mohd Faizal Musa (2015). There is a plethora of works concerning this matter and this point is considered no longer in need of debate. See, for example, Bielefeldt (2020); Oba (2013); Sen (1997); Ishay (2004); and Zechenter (1997).

relationship with Anwar Ibrahim, who had already joined UMNO at the time of publication of his book.

However, while Al-Attas' rejection of secularism might have benefited Islamist groups such as PAS, his rejection of secularism was not moderate, and has had a negative impact on other issues. For example, Shaharuddin Maaruf (2005, p. 324), in his article on "Religion and Utopian Thinking Among the Muslims of Southeast Asia" argued that it had only served to make Muslims disconnected from the history and culture of the region:

> In raising the scare of secularism or secularisation among Muslims, which is seen as the process of dereligionising them, utopian thinking draws the anti-thesis between sacred or divine history and secular or objective natural history. The religion of Islam is identified with the former, while Christianity is tragically portrayed as the latter. Through the anti-thesis of divine history and secular history and the identification of Islam with the former, utopian thinking banished Muslims from the world of action and precluded them from developing existential consciousness of their human conditions in history and the real world they live in. Consequently, Muslims are plucked out of history, they are rendered ahistorical and they are deprived of the legitimacy for self-determinism.

Al-Attas' ideas on secularism also left a strong mark on intellectuals and cultural activists. Azhar Ibrahim (2016) provided a clear explanation on this matter:

> The spectre of secularism in Malay discourse began with Syed Muhammad Naguib Al-Attas' lecture and publication of *Islam and Secularism*. This dismissal and condemnation of secularism made vis-a-vis deliberating on the authentic Islamic approach became ever more popular, and later on, was repeated continuously by many writers and scholars, especially in the discourse of Islam in the Malaysia-Singapore-Brunei context. As there are close cultural and intellectual connections between these Malay-

Muslim societies, it is surprising that secularism became the prime target amongst the revivalists, although theoretically speaking Al-Attas' affiliation is more traditionalistic than revivalist in stance and tenor. Secularism becomes an antithesis to authentic Islam, which is deemed as a holistic system or way of life that can be the antidote for all modern frailties and excesses. It is interesting to note that while Al-Attas' discussion on secularism is an epistemic concern, his ideas have been appropriated by those who have their own political interest in the establishment of an Islamic state; though it is very clear that Al-Attas hardly made any reference for the establishment of an Islamic political entity.

Beyond history and culture, there was Ahmad Fuad Rahmat (2013, p. 83) who argued that Al-Attas' book and ideas on Islamization provided a basis for the rejection of human rights:

A closer reading of *Islam and Secularism* shows it is not the West that Al-Attas has problems with per se, but the values of democratic equality and individual liberty of the modern secular age that emerged triumphant in the West—values which assume some form of natural equality among individuals. Needless to say, this directly contravenes the hierarchy-imbued framework of *adab*[10] that Al-Attas endorses. It is little wonder that the book has been of such value for conservative Muslim politics in Malaysia:

---

[10] *Adab*, an Arabic word which literally translates to "behaviour", also refers to a prescribed Islamic etiquette. Al-Attas argues that *adab* is an important component of Islamic education and defines it as follows: "*Adab* is the discipline of body, mind and soul; the discipline that assures the recognition and acknowledgement of one's proper place in relation to one's physical, intellectual and spiritual capacities and potentials; the recognition and acknowledgement of the reality that knowledge and being are ordered hierarchically according to their various levels and degrees." Put differently, it is a method of knowing by which an individual actualizes the condition of being in its proper place. Al-Attas also adds that *adab* is a reflection of wisdom and a spectacle of justice which is worn by a learned individual. See Al-Attas (1999), p. 22.

the Professor's ideas can be readily used to argue against human rights and the freedom of religious minorities, among many other things.

This rejection of modern human rights can be further observed in his attitude towards equality, which is the foremost component of modern human rights. He referred to the inculcation of equality as an act of "levelling", and an act of ignorance:

> The chief characteristic symptom of loss of *adab* within the Community is the process of *levelling* that is cultivated from time to time in the Muslim mind and practised in his society. By "levelling" I mean the levelling of everyone, in the mind and the attitude, to the same level of the leveller. This mental and attitudinal process, which impinges upon action, is perpetrated through the encouragement of false leaders who wish to demolish legitimate authority and valid hierarchy so that they and their like might thrive, and who demonstrate by example by levelling the great to the level of the less great, and then to that of the still lesser (Al-Attas 1978, p. 104).[11]

Again, Ahmad Fuad Rahmat (2013, p. 97) warned that "levelling" was problematic for a plural and democratic society like Malaysia:

---

[11] He further said that "this Jahili streak of individualism, of immanent arrogance and obstinacy and the tendency to challenge and belittle legitimate authority, seems to have perpetrated itself—albeit only among extremists of many sorts—in all periods of Muslim history. When Muslims become confused in their knowledge of Islam and its world view, these extremists tend to spread among them and influence their thinking and infiltrate into positions of religious leadership; then their leadership in all spheres of life tends to exhibit this dangerous streak and to encourage its practice among Muslims as if it were in conformity with the teachings of Islam." Al-Attas also rejected the concept of freedom as another trait of W stern secularism, arguing that the act of choosing between good and evil should not be allowed. Freedom, according to him, should not be traded "with truth, true and real nature." See Al-Attas (2007), p. 63.

To show that modern secular life and values are enveloped by confusion and a deep divorce from the transcendent enables Al-Attas to argue that man is simply not fit for self-determination. His claim that the secular conception of the autonomous man is a failed project allows him to justify his rejection of equality as a political value and this becomes a pretext for him to assert the necessity of religious hierarchy. This is most evident in how he speaks of modern notions of political equality as "levelling", as an injustice in light of the hierarchy he wishes to uphold.

Recently, conservative groups in Malaysia have used this idea of a "loss of *adab*" to dismiss and to silence growing grievances with regard to Perikatan Nasional's (PN) mishandling of the COVID-19 pandemic.[12]

ISLAMIZATION OF KNOWLEDGE IN EDUCATION

The term Islamization was first coined by Gaafar Syeikh Idris in his pamphlet "The Process of Islamization" which was presented to a conference attended by Muslim students studying in the United States in Toledo, Ohio in 1975. Wan Mohd Nor (2007, p. 72) said that it was this pamphlet that first gave Al-Attas inspiration to conceptualize his ideas on Islamization and to eventually give it a definition and a clear methodology. He then presented his ideas at the international level during the First World Conference on Muslim Education held in Mecca in 1977.[13] Soon after, Al-Attas (1980) proposed Islamization of knowledge in his book, *The Concept of Education in Islam: A Framework for an Islamic Philosophy of Education*, published by ABIM. It is also important to

---

[12] In the midst of growing demands from social media users calling upon the King to address Prime Minister Muhyiddin Yassin's incompetency in handling the pandemic, conservative groups reminded people that the Malay Rulers should not be criticized. See Adila Sharinni Wahid (2021) and Juliana Johar (2021).

[13] Other than Al-Attas, Ismail Raji Al-Faruqi and Seyyed Hossein Nasr also attended the Mecca conference and presented their versions of the Islamization of knowledge. See Abaza (2000), p. 59.

note here that Al-Attas was not the only scholar who had called for the Islamization of knowledge in Muslim society. Other scholars associated with the Islamization of knowledge are Seyyed Hossein Nasr, Ismail Faruqi, Louay Safi, Taha Jabir Alwani and Ibrahim A. Ragab, all of whom emphasized different aspects of the concept.[14]

Al-Attas posited that there are two steps to the Islamization of knowledge. The first, which focuses more on values and thinking, is to de-Westernize and desecularize knowledge, or to replace it with Islamic values and its worldview. This would entail a specific emphasis on the social sciences. The second step, which is more operational, would be the Islamization of language and the infusion of the Islamic worldview into all branches of knowledge (Mohamed Aslam Haneef 2005, pp. 36–37).[15] In *The Concept of Education in Islam*, Al-Attas stated that this infusion cannot be done by merely studying and teaching Islamic concepts, but that it should be done through the establishment of an Islamic institute of learning specially dedicated to the Islamization of knowledge.

In discussing such an institute and the proposed changes to education, Wan Mohd Nor stated that all social science and humanities taught in higher institutions should be cleansed of "the spirit [and] cultural identity [of] modern Western civilization" (Wan Mohd Nor Wan Daud 2007, p. 73).[16] He also suggested that students sit for at least one course

---

[14] Mohamed Aslam Haneef has done a comparison of these scholars, with the exception of Syed Hossein Nasr. See Mohamed Aslam Haneef (2005).

[15] For a summary on this operational framework, see Al-Attas' own writing: Al-Attas (2007). It was first published as part of a collection of papers presented at a conference in 2003. See *Isu dan Proses Pembukaan Minda Umat Melayu Islam* (2003).

[16] Mashitah Sulaiman et al. (2017) claim that the Islamization of knowledge led to the introduction of Islamic education in kindergartens established by ABIM, who had close relations with Al-Attas and Anwar Ibrahim in the 1970s and 1980s: "Islamisation of knowledge which emphasises a new concept of the integrated education system has contributed to the existence of a systematic integrated education institution pioneered by ABIM with the establishment of the first pre-school education TASKI (known as Taman Asuhan Kanak-Kanak Islam) in 1979, Islamic Primary School (SRI—Sekolah Rendah Islam) in 1988, Islamic Secondary School (SMI—Sekolah Menengah Islam) in 1988. The introduction of

on Islamic thought, history and culture every year. This proposal first materialized at the Institute of Malay Language, Literature and Culture (now the Institute of the Malay World and Civilization, or ATMA) in the early 1970s, and later on at ISTAC (Mohamed Aslam Haneef 2005, p. 36). Al-Attas' proposal on the Islamization of knowledge also led to the establishment of the International Islamic University in Kuala Lumpur (Abaza 2015, p. 59).

ISLAMIZATION OF KNOWLEDGE IN LANGUAGE AND LITERATURE

Al-Attas' influence over time goes way beyond the field of education, and I argue that it has had a clear impact on Malay language and literature. More specifically, it has caused Malay literature to lose its non-Malay and non-Muslim readers, and consequently, its role as a bridge between Malaysians of all walks of life. This is because the literature that has been written in line with the idea of Islamization tends to be laden with Islamic elements and is no longer relatable to non-Malay and non-Muslim readers.

As mentioned earlier, Al-Attas proposed that the Islamization of knowledge start with an understanding of the Islamic worldview, which he said would be best accessed through language and literature. This is evident in his paper presented at the National Culture Congress in 1971, where he stressed that Islam was the main source, the strength, and the foundation of Malay literature.[17] He further emphasized that Malay was

---

Islamic education then became the national education policy when the National Education Philosophy was implemented in 1987 as a result of ABIM activists' effort to bring ABIM's philosophy in education at the mainstream level." (p. 913).

[17] According to Al-Attas, Islam should be the only source and framework for Malay literature, thus conceptualizing and contextualizing Malay literature as Islamic. He said that "the recognition that Islam is an important foundation in the matter of the origins of Malay language and literature must now be clearly affirmed and not neglected because if we continue to slumber in ignorance in matters relating to Islam, ignorance of the reality that Islam is the true source of our culture, then we have and will commit a great lie against history, and we alone will incur an infinite loss."

an "Islamic language" (ibid, p. 5).[18] This provided context as to why Al-Attas had a deep interest in Sufism and Hamzah Fansuri, and how his ideas may be misconstrued by his followers to mean that Malay could become a language for exclusive Islamic use.

Two of the most prominent individuals who have promoted Al-Attas' views in the field of Malay literature are Mohd Affandi Hassan and Ungku Maimunah Tahir, both part of a group that promotes *Persuratan Baru*—a Genuine Literature to replace existing fictional concepts in Islam.[19] Proponents and opponents of Genuine Literature continue to have debates with one another till the present day.

Some contend that the concept of Genuine Literature made its way to neighbouring Singapore too. Mohd Affandi noted:

> I was informed, Isa Kamari can be said to know what Genuine Literature is, and once told Siti Aisyah Binti Mohd Salim who wrote her Master's thesis entitled "Alternative History in the Novel Duka Tuan Bertakhta: An Analysis According to the Idea of a Genuine Literature" (UKM, 2014) to study his novel using a Genuine Literature approach. Siti Aisyah even copied a note from her Facebook which says "I personally want someone to analyse Duka Tuan Bertakhta from the perspective of Genuine

---

[18] In his presentation, Al-Attas referred to Malay as an Islamic language. He said that "the Malay language should be regarded as an Islamic language and must be grouped with the history of Islamic culture, just as Malay literature should be understood as Islamic literature."

[19] Another strong advocate of the idea is Mohd Zariat Abdul Rani, who is based at Universiti Putra Malaysia (UPM). For more discussion on Genuine Literature, see Mohd Faizal Musa (2021). According to Wan Ahmad Fayhsal (2009a), "the idea of a Genuine Literature is an Islamization of Malay Literary Knowledge Project" and he hopes "there will be more supporters of this idea so as to save the literary world from the plague of secularism." The basic ideas of this Genuine Literature by Mohd Affandi are said to be "based on the thought of Al-Attas" (Mohd Ali Atan 2009). In order to understand the root of this idea, we should revisit Al-Attas' (1971, p. 5) presentation at the National Culture Congress.

Literature." This request sounds very foreign to Malaysian writers who can be said to be more or less against knowledge and against the idea of Genuine Literature.

Isa Kamari is a renowned Singaporean writer of Malay literature who was honoured with the S.E.A Write Award in 2006 and the Cultural Medallion in 2007.

Starting with a rejection of secularism, this group proposed Genuine Literature as an antidote to the concept of fictionality which they argued was an imitation of Western art (Mohd Affandi Hassan 1992, p. 24). They denigrated writers who used a Western mould and claimed that Genuine Literature was more authentic. All of this was done based on the writings of Al-Attas (Ungku Maimunah Mohd Tahir 2009, pp. 72–77). For example, in her inaugural lecture of appointment as professor, Ungku Maimunah said that Hamzah Fansuri was far worthier to be given the title of "Father of Malay Literature" than Munshi Abdullah who was merely an "officer of the British administration, Christian missionary and a person of the West" (Ungku Maimunah 2007, p. 20). Al-Attas first made this argument about Hamzah Fansuri at the National Culture Congress in 1971 and continued to do so in subsequent publications.

In trying to promote a Genuine Literature based on Al-Attas' ideas, Mohd Affandi (*Mingguan Malaysia*, 29 January 2006) argued that writers who used the mould of Genuine Literature were those who wrote the truly knowledgeable works of literature, while those who chose a story mould were to be regarded as writers of fiction and were without any value. He also chastised critics of Malay literature as shams (*Mingguan Malaysia*, 20 November 2005). This provoked polemics from other writers. For example, Abdul Rahim Abdullah, the former literary editor of *Berita Harian*, responded by saying that "Affandi seems to rudely force people to accept his theories. If a person writes a creative piece of work and does not use his foundation of knowledge, or if his theory is void, then the work is morally cheap" (*Mingguan Malaysia*, 18 December 2005). Abdul Rahim also disputed Affandi's reference to Al-Attas. He said:

If Affandi takes the idol Syed Naquib as the trigger for his initial theory, which was later expanded or modified by Affandi, he should have learnt a lesson from his teacher; Syed Naquib never lashed out and attacked people (figures) who were not in line with him. From there only will people respect the level and status of one's knowledge. In other words, this method of teaching and imparting knowledge actually requires strict manners, and cannot use reckless emotions and sentiments. This is what I mean, that Affandi is confused about the scientific tradition (if you follow the discipline of Islam and Malay cultural values).

Based on these examples, Al-Attas' ideas on Islamization clearly had an impact on the Malay literary scene.

However, Al-Attas' views on Islamization go beyond just literature, and are also applicable to language use. For example, he supported the idea that certain Arabic terms adopted by Malay, should only be used by Muslims, since Arabic and Malay were both Islamic languages.[20] In a Facebook post from 28 December 2012, Al-Attas used this argument to rebuke claims by the local Christian community that they should also be allowed to use the world "Allah" to refer to God:

> Well I have been talking about this long time ago. I remember about this in ISTAC, when we first established ourselves (late 80s and early 90s), I think the Archbishop of Penang was asking

---

[20] Although Al-Attas did not list specific terms or words, he dedicated a chapter in *Tinjauan Ringkas Peri Ilmu dan Pandangan Alam* (*A Brief Overview of Knowledge and Weltanschauung*) (2007, pp. 47–62) to argue from a philosophical perspective that certain words in Malay and Arabic share the same foundation in relation to Islam and the Qur'an, thus justifying that there are words which are to be used exclusively by Muslims. For example, that non-Muslims cannot use the word "Allah". He also claimed that a non-Islamic perspective and outlook has been used to define and understand the spirit of Islamic terms. He said that "many of the keywords from basic Islamic terminology which are used in various languages by Muslims have become obscure because they have been arbitrarily used to serve other disciplines, which is akin to a decline towards non-Islamic worldviews; a phenomenon which I call the denial of Islam in language" (ibid, p. 60). He also referred to those who adopt foreign outlooks to understand key Islamic terms as confused smugglers who have shallow knowledge. "*Weltanschauung*" refers to "worldview".

this question. And I have answered that. And then we had a meeting with the Archbishop of Kuala Lumpur and about all the representatives of Christianity, including the ministers, we had a meeting at ISTAC. And I said, "Why you want to use the word 'Allah' for yourself?" They said "we going to pray in Bahasa Malaysia." That's the way they put it. So my answers to them, "Why you have to change praying into Bahasa Malaysia. You have been praying in English all the time. Why suddenly change into Bahasa Malaysia?" OK, so they said they want to change so that it more patriotic. Then in that case I'm saying that "why don't you use Tuhan while praying in Bahasa Malaysia? Because you are talking about God isn't it? ... God is not just a name ... 'Allah' is a name of this Being whom you called God ... and in fact a Being whom even higher than what you called to be God" And then I said, "... and 'Allah' is not from Bahasa Malaysia. It is not a national language. It belongs to the language of Muslim all over the world. Therefore your argument using this for the word 'Allah' does not fit into your idea of God. Because 'Allah' does not have a son, It is not one of three (Trinity), that is why out of respect to Allah we can't allow you to use this."[21]

This view is supported by conservative Muslim groups, including the religious establishment and right-wing Malay organizations in the country.[22] The exact quotation above once again made its rounds in March 2021 when the Kuala Lumpur High Court quashed a ruling which banned Christians from using "Allah" in their publications.[23] I argue that this is one of the many examples which illustrate how Al-Attas' Islamization of knowledge has been applied by exclusivists to fan antagonism between Muslims and non-Muslims in Malaysia.

---

[21] See Al-Attas (2012).

[22] See Mufti of Federal Territory (2017). See also Siti Hafidah (2021). ISMA is a well-known right-wing Malay organization.

[23] See Lim (2021).

AL-ATTAS' STUDENTS, FOLLOWERS AND FANS IN THE MAINSTREAM

As discussed earlier, Al-Attas' conception of Islamization involves the denouncement of secularism and the West. Despite the fact that his blatant criticisms are not moderate, his views on Islam and secularism have gained traction among his followers. Additionally, his vision of the Islamization of knowledge is also well celebrated by his former students.[24]

Among the scholars considered as Al-Attas' protégés are those who had him as their mentor when he was based at ISTAC. These include Wan Mohd Nor Wan Daud, Khalif Muammar (Centre for Advanced Studies on Islam, Science and Civilization, CASIS-UTM), Zainiy Uthman (International Islamic University Malaysia, IIUM), Farid Shahran (former leader of ABIM; IIUM), Wan Suhaimi Wan Abdullah (UM), Azizan Sabjan (Universiti Sains Malaysia, USM), as well as Indonesian graduates such as Syamsuddin Arif, Hamid Fahmy Zarkasyi, Adian Husaini, Adnin Armas, and Ugi Suharto.[25]

As has been discussed by Farish Noor, Mona Abaza, Ahmad Fuad Rahmat, and Ahmad Fauzi, Al-Attas played an important role in the Islamization process sponsored by the Malaysian government. For example, when Anwar Ibrahim was in the government, Al-Attas and his students benefited from Mahathir Mohamad's administration.[26] During

---

[24] It is impossible here not to mention the late Syed Hussein Alatas, the brother of Syed Naquib Al-Attas. In my opinion, both of them have opposing ideas on the betterment of society. Mona Abaza summarizes the differences between both of them in her work. See Abaza (2005), p. 238. See Alatas (1988), p. 14.

[25] Al-Attas' students and followers go beyond those who studied under him or were supervised by him. Even when he was based in UKM from 1971 to 1972, he actively engaged with undergraduates who were not necessarily his students, and these engagements also happened in his own home. Thus, his influence was not just limited to his "formal students". See Mashitah Sulaiman et al. (2017), p. 913.

[26] According to Ahmad Fauzi, Al-Attas and his students were highly utilized by the government in the 1980s and 1990s: "Al-Attas' discourse became a tool to legitimize the Islamist initiatives of the Malaysian state under Dr Mahathir's premiership (1981–2003), particularly during the years of Anwar Ibrahim as minister of education (1987–91) and deputy prime minister (1994–98)." See Ahmad Fauzi Abdul Hamid (2018), p. 377.

Abdullah Ahmad Badawi's subsequent administration, the students or followers of Al-Attas were given a role in shaping government policy, especially when it came to the conceptualization of Islam Hadhari:

> The concept of Islam Hadhari is also linked to the Malaysian government's new approach to addressing the post-Islamic revivalism era which witnessed the Muslim ummah facing the pressures of a Western-sponsored globalization agenda. This intention was also translated into human development programmes, especially for public servants and the application of Islamic values in a training programme conducted by INTAN which was strengthened with the help of several renowned Malay-Muslim intellectuals such as Kamal Hassan, Syed Naquib Al-Attas, Wan Mohd Nor Wan Daud and others. The aspect of human development is the main core in giving birth to a society which is intellectual, skilled and virtuous. This can be seen implicitly in the idea of Islam Hadhari (Adam Bin Badrulhisham and Mohamad Firdaus bin Mohd Isa 2017, p. 193).

Al-Attas' former students' engagement with the government continued under the administration of Mohd Najib Razak. It was during this time that they became very central in the government, serving in the National Civics Bureau (BTN).[27] For example, in June 2011, Wan Mohd Nor, who was then the director of CASIS, was appointed honorary fellow at the National Academy of the BTN. The appointment, according to the Director General of the BTN at the time, Raja Arif Raja Ali, allowed him to "give advice and help to intensify activities to inculcate a patriotic spirit, in line with the BTN's desire to make the academy an excellent training centre" (*Mstar*, 11 August 2011). In fulfilment of his role in the BTN, he published a short book titled *Budaya Ilmu dan Gagasan 1Malaysia:*

---

[27] The National Civics Bureau (Biro Tata Negara, BTN) is an agency under the Prime Minister's Department whose role is to conduct programmes for civil servants and politicians. Mohd Najib Razak's arguments about human rights are in line with the views of Al-Attas. See Ong Han Sean (2014).

Membina Negara Maju dan Bahagia (*The Culture of Knowledge and the 1Malaysia Vision: Building a Prosperous and Happy Nation*). In this book, Wan Mohd Nor realigns Al-Attas' ideas by trying to apply them to the 1Malaysia vision. In doing so, he rejects any attempt to justify liberalization and equality on the grounds that Malaysia needs its own and more holistic framework for prosperity and happiness. Coincidently, it was under Najib Razak's administration that book banning arose, especially books by those considered to be promoting liberal and human rights. Under the current PN government, Al-Attas' students continue to be a part of the mainstream in that at least two individuals who have claimed to be his students hold the positions of deputy minister and minister, therefore having a say in policy-making activities.[28]

Others who claim to be followers of Al-Attas compare their idol to other prominent Islamists. For example, Ugi Suharto, one of Al-Attas' students from Indonesia (2002, p. 164), sees many similarities between Al-Attas and Al-Qaradhawi, the leader of the Muslim Brotherhood in Qatar and Egypt:

> Al-Attas as a true Muslim thinker, and Al-Qaradhawi as an authoritative Muslim jurist, both agree that secularism is not only contrary to Islam, but is even against Islam. The sensitivity of both Muslim scholars to this fundamental problem of the *ummah*, at the same time shows that the issue of secularism should not be taken lightly by Muslims themselves. The dangers of secularism and secularization, and their processes, whether at the individual or national level, should make us even more wary of the ideologies that accompany them, even though they have the same name and new "clothes", such as the understanding of change, globalization, development and others.

---

[28] In a 2009 blog post by Wan Ahmad Fayhsal titled "Meeting Prof. Dr Syed Muhammad Naquib Al-Attas", he explains his admiration for Al-Attas. He also notes that Saifuddin Abdullah, who at that time was the Deputy Minister for High r Education in Malaysia, "spent a whole day in the inaugural seminar and lecture simply because of his conviction as a student to a teacher whom he greatly benefited from as a human being" (Wan Ahmad Fayhsal 2009c).

It should be noted here that Ugi (2002, p. 143) stated in his paper that he had consulted with Al-Attas and Wan Mohd Nor when he drew the comparison between Al-Attas and Al-Qaradhawi. This is interesting considering the fact that Al-Attas has been referred to as a neo-traditionalist because he "tended to mix Sufism with the philosophy of the Islamic sciences" (Komaruddin Sassi 2020, p. 69), while Al-Qaradhawi is mainly associated with the Muslim Brotherhood.[29]

This relationship between the followers of Al-Attas and other conservative Islamic groups becomes more apparent when they are compared with INSISTS,[30] a collective of academics and former graduates from Indonesia who studied at ISTAC:

> The choice of conservatism can be seen from how INSISTS formulates its vision, mission, and objectives, namely, to clarify and reformulate the methodology of Islamic thought and civilization that is relevant to the problems faced by Muslims, such as in the fields of science, education, history, civilization, politics, economics, social, and gender equality. INSISTS activists appear to be critical of all interpretations—both classical and traditional, even against establishment—and anti-liberal thinking. In their eyes, the Western Orientalist approach must be critically reviewed. The choice of conservatism—as van Bruinessen views it—seems inseparable from the influence of their teachers in Malaysia, namely Syed Naquib Al-Attas. In their various writings,

---

[29] To understand neo-traditionalism in the Malaysian context, see Ahmad Fauzi Abdul Hamid (2019). Also included in this group apart from Al-Attas are Abdullah bin Bayyah, Sheikh Umar Faruq Abd-Allah, and Hamza Yusuf who is close to Al-Attas. See also *Berita Harian Online*, 8 June 2016.

[30] It is akin to an Indonesian branch of Al-Attas followers. Syukur (2018, p. 148) states that "the organization, INSISTS, was established on 4 March 2003 in Segambut Village, Kuala Lumpur, Malaysia, by collaborating students and lecturers from the Indonesian Institute of Islamic Thought and Civilization (ISTAC) who share the idea of building a civilization based on an Islamic worldview. When its activities began to spread in Indonesia, the activists involved in the INSISTS study then formed the 'INSISTS network', which began to emerge in 2008."

there is a great respect for the figure of Al-Attas, because of his intelligence, consistency and high morality. The results of the thoughts and ideas of Al-Attas about "Islamization of science" and *adab* were then received into Indonesia, even contextualized in the Indonesian situation (Syukur 2018, p. 149).

As evident from the paragraph above, Al-Attas' project to de-Westernize society and to implement the Islamization of knowledge was also adopted, promoted, and popularized by his followers in Indonesia.

Although Al-Attas and his followers are considered elitist and detached from the masses, their approach to befriend the establishment put the Islamization of knowledge at a focal point. As Mona Abaza (2015, p. 62) put it, "the promoters of this discourse could be viewed as attempting to enhance a new bureaucratic elite in Malaysia. The promoters of the 'Islamization of knowledge debate' are in the centre of power and are spokesmen of the Malaysian government's vision of Islam. They hold significant positions in academic, publishing and government offices."

CONCLUSION

When it was first introduced, Al-Attas' Islamization of knowledge might have simply been a response to the Islamic revivalism that began in the 1970s. Despite Komaruddin Sassi's (2020, p. 258) conclusion that Al-Attas' Islamization of knowledge lacked the dynamic needed to extend its life beyond its present form, the concept and phenomenon have gained traction and have evolved to become a threat to Malaysia's heterogeneous society and socio-political fabric, and this is evident from the impact it has had on education and culture in Malaysia.

Furthermore, in the wake of the Wahhabi punitive attitude that has been gaining ground in Malaysia since the 1980s, this project appears to provide conservative Muslim groups with more ammunition to criticize, veil, and even ban important pre-Islamic Malay intellectual heritage and cultural practices.[31] The style of thinking underlying Wahhabism—a

---

[31] The International Islamic University of Malaysia (IIUM), under which ISTAC operates, was funded by Saudi petro dollars. See Mohd Faizal Musa (2018b).

brand of Islam from Saudi Arabia that constructs the world in terms of Islamic and non-Islamic, and glorifying Islamic past—is shared by Islamization of knowledge proponents. Wahhabism, which is an exclusivist and puritanical brand of Islam, antagonizes older traditions and frequently alienates doctrines and practices which it deems to be heretic or which are referred to as innovations. It could be argued that the goals of Al-Attas' Islamization of knowledge and the undermining of Hindu-Buddhist influence on pre-Islamic Malay culture exhibit similar reasoning, albeit that Al-Attas may reject Wahhabism's attitude towards Sufism.[32]

Over time, Al-Attas' followers have become part of mainstream Islam in Malaysia as they have leveraged on state machinery and government agencies to continue operating. They also use the platforms of culture and education to spread their ideas, and can be argued to be elitist and conservative. Interestingly, proponents of *"ketuanan Melayu-Islam"* (Malay-Islamic supremacy) have also based their struggle on Al-Attas' critique of secularism. More writings and reflections from others scholars are needed in order to analyse the impact of Al-Attas' ideas in the fields of education and culture. Meanwhile, contemporary scholars should do more to bring balance to the discourse on Islam. For example, Syed Hussein Alatas' writings on progressive Islam should be resurrected to counteract the exclusivist tendencies of the Islamization of knowledge project.

Acknowledgement

First of all, I would like to thank Sharifah Afra Alatas for her tremendous help while writing this piece. Also, I am indebted to Professor Dr Syed Farid Alatas bin Syed Hussein Alatas, Associate Professor Dr Noor Aisha binti Abdul Rahman, Dr Shaharuddin bin Maaruf and Dr Azhar Ibrahim for their invaluable comments and critical inputs.

---

[32] See also Mohd Faizal Musa and Siti Syazwani Zainal Abidin (2021).

REFERENCES

A. Kadir Jasin. 2020. "Jangan Cuba Berselindung di Sebalik Tragedi Ali-Muawiyah". *Malaysiakini*, 1 April 2020. https://www.malaysiakini.com/news/518073

A. Rahim Abdullah. 2005. "Affandi Keliru Tradisi Ilmu". *Mingguan Malaysia*, 18 December 2005.

Abaza, Mona. 1999. "Intellectuals, Power and Islam in Malaysia: S.N. Al-Attas or the Beacon on the Crest of a Hill". *Archipel* 58: 189–217.

———. 2000. "The Islamization of Knowledge between Particularism and Globalization: Malaysia and Egypt". In *Situating Globalization: Views from Egypt*, edited by Cynthia Nelson and Shahnaz Rouse, pp. 53–96. Bielefeld: transcript Verlag.

———. 2005. "Syed Hussein Alatas and Progressive Islam Between The Middle East and Southeast Asia". In *Local and Global Social Transformation in Southeast Asia: Essays in Honour of Professor Syed Hussein Alatas*, edited by Riaz Hassan, pp. 237–60. Kuala Lumpur: Dewan Bahasa dan Pustaka.

Abdul Razak Ayub. 1985. *Perpecahan Bangsa Melayu*. Shah Alam: Dewan Pustaka Fajar.

Abdul Rahman Embong. 2002. "Malaysia as a Multicultural Society". *Macalester International* 12, no. 10: 37–58.

Adam Bin Badhrulhisham and Mohamad Firdaus bin Mohd Isa. 2017. "Islamisasi Negara Malaysia Dalam Konteks Gagasan Islamisasi Ilmu Syed Muhammad Naquib Al-'Attas: Satu Tinjauan". *Jurnal Ulwan* 1: 189–203. https://kuim.edu.my/journal/index.php/JULWAN/article/viewFile/186/165

Adila Sharinni Wahid. 2021. "Hina Agong: PAS Kelantan Gesa Tindakan Tegas". *Sinar Harian*, 1 June 2021. https://www.sinarharian.com.my/article/141531/BERITA/Politik/Hina-Agong-Pas-Kelantan-gesa-tindakan-tegas

Ahmad Fauzi Abdul Hamid. 2010. *Islamic Education in Malaysia*. RSIS Monograph no. 18. Singapore: Rajaratnam School of International Studies.

———. 2018. "Shifting Trends of Islamism and Islamist Practices in Malaysia, 1957–2017". *Southeast Asian Studies* 7, no. 3: 363–90.

————. 2019. "Neo Traditionalist Islam in Malaysia: Neither Salafi Nor Traditionalist". *The Asia Dialogue*, 8 May 2019. https://theasiadialogue.com/2019/05/08/neo-traditionalist-islam-in-malaysia-neither-salafi-nor-traditionalist/

Ahmad Fuad Rahmat. 2013. "The Professor and The Secular". *Critical Muslim* 7: 81–100.

Alatas, Syed Hussein. 1968. "Feudalism in Malaysian Society: A Study in Historical Continuity". *Civilisations* 18, no. 4: 579–92.

————. 1988. "Kita Runtuh Akhlak dan Kurang Berfikir". *Dewan Budaya* (June), pp. 9–17.

Al-Attas, Syed Muhammad Naquib. 1971. "Prosiding Kongres Kebudayaan Malaysia: Kertas Kerja 5". Seminar Dasar: Nilai-Nilai Kebudayaan Dalam Bahasa dan Kesusasteraan Melayu, 18 August 1971. Bilik Kuliah Ekonomi A, Universiti Malaya.

————. 1978. *Islam and Secularism*. Kuala Lumpur: ABIM.

————. 1980. *The Concept of Education in Islam: A Framework for an Islamic Philosophy of Education*. Kuala Lumpur: Angkatan Belia Islam Malaysia.

————. 1999. *The Concept of Education in Islam: A Framework for an Islamic Philosophy of Education*. Kuala Lumpur: ISTAC.

————. 2001. *Risalah untuk Kaum Muslimin*. Kuala Lumpur: International Institute of Islamic Thought and Civilization.

————. 2003. "Tinjauan Ringkas Peri Ilmu dan Pandangan Alam". In *Isu dan Proses Pembukaan Minda Umat Melayu Islam*, by Panel Penulis. Kuala Lumpur: Dewan Bahasa dan Pustaka.

————. 2007. *Tinjauan Ringkas Peri Ilmu dan Pandangan Alam (A Brief Overview of Knowledge and Weltanschauung)*. Penang: Penerbit Universiti Sains Malaysia.

————. 2011. *Historical Fact and Fiction*. Skudai: Penerbit UTM Press.

————. 2012. *Facebook*, 28 December 2012. https://m.facebook.com/permalink.php?story_fbid=571149779569031&id=193058140711532&locale2=hi_IN

Aqil Fithri. 2010. "Tiada Lagi Label Isu Sensitif". *Malaysiakini*, 31 August 2010. https://www.malaysiakini.com/news/141548

Azhar Ibrahim. 2016. "Secularism as Imagined in the Malay-Indonesian

World: Resistance and its Muted Counter Responses in the Discursive and Public Realms". *Islamic Renaissance Front*, 3 June 2016. https://irfront.net/post/articles/secularism-as-imagined-in-the-malay-indonesian-world-resistance-and-its-muted-counter-responses-in-the-discursive-and-public-realms/

Berita Harian Online. 2016. "Pegang Akidah Ahli Sunnah Wal Jamaah". 8 June 2016. https://www.bharian.com.my/bhplus-old/2016/06/161920/pegang-akidah-ahli-sunnah-wal-jamaah

————. 2018. "Buku Tegaskan Islam Bukan Penumpang di Alam Melayu". 23 February 2018. https://www.bharian.com.my/rencana/sastera/2018/02/391896/buku-tegaskan-islam-bukan-penumpang-di-alam-melayu

Bielefeldt, Heiner. 2000. "'Western' versus 'Islamic' Human Rights Conceptions? A Critique of Cultural Essentialism in the Discussion on Human Rights". *Political Theory* 28, no. 1: 90–121.

Farish A. Noor. 2004. *Islam Embedded: The Historical Development of the Pan-Malaysian Islamic Party PAS (1951–2003)*. Kuala Lumpur: Malaysian Sociological Research Institute.

Hasanul Arifin Zawawi. 2013. "The Malay Language and Its Role in Nation Building: Summary of Saturday Night Lecture 14th September 2013. Summary of Saturday Night Lecture 3rd Series with SMN Al-Attas". *UTM CASIS Blog*. 14 September 2013. https://www.utm.my/casis/blog/2013/09/24/the-malay-language-and-its-role-in-nation-building-summary-of-saturday-night-lecture-14th-september-2013/

Hashim Haji Musa. 2006. "Merekonstruksi Tamadun Melayu Islam Ke Arah Pembinaan Sebuah Tamadun Dunia Alaf Ketiga". In *Melayu Islam dan Pendidikan*, edited by Hashim Yaacob and Hamedi Mohd Adnan, pp. 15–89. Kuala Lumpur: Penerbit Universiti Malaya.

Ishay, Micheline R. 2004. "What Are Human Rights? Six Historical Controversies". *Journal of Human Rights* 3, no. 3: 359–71.

Isu dan Proses Pembukaan Minda Umat Melayu Islam. 2003. Kuala Lumpur: Dewan Bahasa dan Pustaka.

Juliana Johar. 2021. "Noor Kartini Mohon Maaf Kepada Sultan Johor, Tunku Idris Pula Berkongsi Tentang Adab". *MStar*, 30 May 2021, https://www.mstar.com.my/spotlight/hiburan/2021/05/30/

ibu-neelofa-mohon-maaf-kepada-sultan-johor-tengku-idris-pula-berkongsi-tentang-adab

Khalif Muammar. 2018. "Ketuanan Melayu Dan Ketuanan Rakyat Dari Perspektif Islam". *Khalif Muammar Wordpress*, 19 April 2018. https://khalifmuammar.wordpress.com/2018/04/19/ketuanan-melayu-dan-ketuanan-rakyat-dari-perspektif-islam/

Komaruddin Sassi. 2020. *Ontologi Pendidikan Islam Paradigma Tauhid Syed Muhammad Naquib Al-Attas: Revitalisasi Adab-Ta'dib Dalam Pendidikan*. Jakarta: Kencana.

Lim, Ida. 2021. "High Court Quashes Govt's 1986 Ban on 'Allah' Use by Christians, Affirms Sarawakian Bumiputera's Right to Religion and Non-Discrimination". *Malay Mail*, 10 March 2021. https://www.malaymail.com/news/malaysia/2021/03/10/high-court-quashes-govts-1986-ban-on-allah-use-by-christians-affirms-sarawa/1956527

Malaysiakini. 2019. "Elemen Gelap Daulah Terpendam Cuba Sabotaj PH—Saifuddin". 30 July 2019. https://www.malaysiakini.com/news/485921

Mashitah Sulaiman, Mohd Nazir Ahmad, Marina Munira Abdul Mutalib, and Roslizawati Mohd Ramly. 2017. "Inculcating Islamic Knowledge Tradition Among the Malays: Malaysian Experience". In Proceedings of the 3rd International Conference on Advances in Education and Social Sciences. Istanbul, 9–11 October 2017, pp. 908–25.

Milner, Anthony. 2011. *The Malays*. West Sussex: Wiley-Blackwell.

Mohamed Aslam Haneef. 2005. *A Critical Survey of Islamization of Knowledge*. Kuala Lumpur: Research Centre International Islamic University Malaysia.

Mohamed Mustafa Ishak. 1999. "From Plural Society to Bangsa Malaysia: Ethnicity and Nationalism in the Politics of Nation-Building in Malaysia". Doctoral Thesis, Department of Sociology and Social Policy and Department of Politics, University of Leeds.

Mohd Affandi Hassan. 1992. *Pendidikan Estetika Daripada Pendekatan Tauhid*. Kuala Lumpur: Dewan Bahasa dan Pustaka.

———. 2005. "Pemikiran Picisan A. Rahim". *Mingguan Malaysia*, 20 November 2005.

————. 2006. "Menguji Kredibiliti Editor". *Mingguan Malaysia*, 29 January 2006.

————. 2018. "Gagasan Persuratan Baru Sebagai Pilihan". *Blog Gagasan Persuratan Baru*, 24 January 2018. http://pbaru.blogspot.com/2018/01/gagasan-persuratan-baru-sebagai-pilihan.html

Mohd Ali Atan. 2009. "Sisi Lain Tentang Sastera". *Utusan Online*, 28 June 2009. https://indahnyasastera.weebly.com/artikel---artikel-sastera.html

Mohd Faizal Musa. 2015. "Pengantar Hak Asasi Manusia Moden dan Hujah Sangkalan Ia Bertentangan Dengan Islam". *International Journal of the Malay World and Civilisation (Iman)* 3, no. 3: 79–94.

————. 2018a. "Human Rights Are Not Western: There Were Similar Concepts in Traditional Malay Society". In *Budi Kritik*, edited by Mohamed Imran Mohamed Taib and Nurul Fadiah Johari, pp. 47–58. Singapore: The Literary Centre and The Reading Group.

————. 2018b. "The Riyal and Ringgit of Petro-Islam: Investing Salafism in Education". In *Islam in Southeast Asia: Negotiating Modernity*, edited by Norshahril Saat, pp. 63–87. Singapore: ISEAS – Yusof Ishak Institute.

————. 2021. "Tanggapan Terhadap Persuratan Baru: Ambiguiti dalam Pujangga Melayu Karya Mohd Affandi Hassan". *Jurnal Antarabangsa Alam dan Tamadun Melayu* 9, no. 1: 29–45.

————, and Siti Syazwani Zainal Abidin. 2021. "Longer Term External Conditions Behind Legal Conservatism in Malaysian Islam". *ISEAS Perspective* no. 2021/23, 4 March 2021, pp. 1–9.

Mohd Hazim Shah Abdul Murad, ed. 2009. *Sains, Agama dan Budaya di Alam Melayu*. Kuala Lumpur: Dewan Bahasa dan Pustaka.

Mstar. 2011. "Dr Wan Mohd Nor Dilantik Felo Kehormat Akademi Kenegaraan". 11 August 2011. https://www.mstar.com.my/lokal/semasa/2011/08/11/dr-wan-mohd-nor-dilantik-felo-kehormat-akademi-kenegaraan

Mufti of Federal Territory. 2017. "Isu Nama ALLAH: Mengapa Orang Bukan Islam Tidak Berhak Menggunakan Nama ALLAH". *Official Website of the Mufti of Federal Territory*, 9 November 2017. https://muftiwp.gov.my/en/sumber/media/penerbitan/suarapemikir/2157-isu-nama-allah-mengapa-orang-bukan-islam-tidak-berhak-menggunakan-nama-allah

Muzaffar, Chandra. 1987. *Islamic Resurgence in Malaysia*. Petaling Jaya: Penerbit Fajar Bakti.

Najibah Abdul Mutalib. 2000. "Pemikiran Teori Ilmu Menurut Syed Muhammad Naquib Al-Attas". *Wacana Dialog Peradaban*: 63–75.

Oba, Abdulmumini A. 2013. "New Muslim Perspectives in the Human Rights Debate". In *Islam and International Law: Engaging Self Centrism from a Plurality of Perspectives*, edited by Marie Luisa Frick and Andreas Th Muller, pp. 217–43. Leiden: Brill.

Ong Han Sean. 2014. "Najib: 'Human Rights-ism' Goes Against Muslim Values". *The Star Online*, 13 May 2014. http://www.thestar.com. my/News/Nation/2014/05/13/Najib-human-rightsism-against-muslim-values/

Ooi Kee Beng. 2012. "Hak Untuk Berbeza Pendapat: Lim Kit Siang Sebuah Lakaran Biografi". Kuala Lumpur: REFSA.

Sen, Amartya. 1997. *Human Rights and Asian Values*. New York: Carnegie Council on Ethics and International Affairs.

Shaharir Mohamad Zain. 2000. "Angka Melayu Sebelum Kedatangan Islam". *Bulletin of the Malaysian Mathematical Sciences Society* 23, no. 2: 187–220.

———. 2003. "The Oldest Known Malay Ethno Science: A Case Study in Malay Ethnobotany Based on a 7th Century Talang Tuwo Inscription and Malay Proverbs". *Malaysian Journal of Science and Technology Studies* 1: 78–113.

Shaharir Mohamad Zain and Zahrin Affandi Mohd Zahrin. 2019. "Sistem Angka Perpuluhan Yang Diketahui Tertua di Dunia: Angka Malayonesia". *Journal of Science and Mathematics Letters* 7: 52–65.

Shaharuddin Maaruf. 2005. "Religion and Utopian Thinking Among the Muslims of Southeast Asia". In *Local and Global Social Transformation in Southeast Asia: Essays in Honour of Professor Syed Hussein Alatas*, edited by Riaz Hassan, pp. 315–30. Kuala Lumpur: Dewan Bahasa dan Pustaka.

———. 2014. *Concept of a Hero in Malay Society*. Petaling Jaya: Strategic Information and Research Development Centre.

Siti Hafidah. 2021. "Mengapa Kristian Bersungguh Ingin Guna Kalimah

Allah?". *ISMAweb*, 11 March 2021. https://ismaweb.net/2021/03/11/mengapa-kristian-bersungguh-ingin-guna-kalimah-allah/

Suharto, Ugi. 2002. "Al-Attas dan al-Qaradawi Mengenai Islam dan Sekularisme". *Afkar-Jurnal Akidah dan Pemikiran Islam*: 143–64.

Syukur, Yanuardi. 2018. "Understanding Terrorism, Peace, and Tolerance from the Institute for the Study of Islam and Civilizations (INSISTS) Activists in Indonesia". *Advances in Social Science, Education and Humanities Research* 365, Second International Conference on Strategic and Global Studies, pp. 148–54.

Ungku Maimumah Mohd Tahir. 2007. *Kritikan Sastera Melayu: Antara Cerita Dengan Ilmu*. Bangi: Penerbit Universiti Kebangsaan Malaysia.

————. 2009. *Dinamika Pemikiran Sastera Melayu*. Kuala Lumpur: Dewan Bahasa dan Pustaka.

Wan Ahmad Fayhsal bin Wan Ahmad Kamal. 2009a. "Sehari Bersama Orang-Orang Sastera dan Polemik Gagasan Persuratan Baru". *Rausyanfikirblog*, 31 May 2009. http://www.rausyanfikir.com/2009/05/sehari-bersama-orang-orang-sastera-dan.html

————. 2009b. "Prof Wan Daud dan Dr Khalif Muammar: 'Powerful Ideas, Salah Satu Sumbangan Naquib Al-Attas'". *Rausyanfikirblog*, 15 July 2009. https://rausyanfikirblog.wordpress.com/2009/07/15/prof-wan-daud-dan-dr-khalif-muammar-powerful-ideas-salah-satu-sumbangan-naquib-al-attas/

————. 2009c. "Bertemu Prof. Dr. Syed Muhammad Naquib Al-Attas". *Rausyanfikirblog*, 14 December 2009. http://www.rausyanfikir.com/2009/12/bertemu-prof-dr-syed-muhammad-naquib-al.html

————. 2014. "Hak dan Tanggungjawab 'Ketuanan Melayu' Tidak Datang Bergolek". *Rausyanfikirblog*, 12 December 2014. http://www.rausyanfikir.com/2014/12/hak-dan-tanggungjawab-ketuanan-melayu.html

Wan Mohd Nor Wan Daud. 2007. *Budaya Ilmu: Satu Penjelasan*. Singapore: Pustaka Nasional.

————. 2011. *Budaya Ilmu Dan Gagasan 1Malaysia: Membina Negara Maju Dan Bahagia*. Kuala Lumpur: Akademi Kenegaraan BTN.

Zechenter, Elizabeth M. 1997. "In the Name of Culture: Cultural Relativism and the Abuse of the Individual". *Journal of Anthropological Research* 53, no. 3: 319–47.